Living Your DREAM

By
Elaine Kule

Modern Curriculum Press

Credits

Photos: All photos © Pearson Learning unless otherwise noted.

Title page: PhotoDisc, Inc. 5: Richard Shock/Liaison International. 6: ©Jerry Watcher/Photo Researchers, Inc. 7: l. Darren Carroll, m. Paul J. Sutton, r. Rick Rickman/Duomo Photography. 8: Brad Mangin/Duomo Photography. 9, 10: Courtesy of Summer Sanders and Her Family. 11: Heinz Kluetmeir/Sports Illustrated Picture Collection. 12: Paul J. Sutton/Duomo Photography. 13: Janette Beckman/Nickelodeon Magazine. 14, 15, 16, 17: Todd Sumlin. 18: Duomo Photography. 19: Ben Van Hook/Duomo Photography. 24: Al Tielemans/Duomo Photography. 25: Jamie Squire/Allsport. 26: Tony Arruza/Corbis. 27, 28: Suzanne Murphy-Larronde. 29: AP/Wide World Photos. 30: Vincent Laforet/Allsport. 31: Chris Trotman/Duomo Photography.

Cover design by Lisa Ann Arcuri

Book design by Lisa Ann Arcuri and Lucie Maragni

ISBN 0-7652-1369-9

Printed in the United States of America

10 11   07 06

Modern Curriculum Press

Pearson Learning Group

1-800-321-3106
www.pearsonlearning.com

CONTENTS

To everyone with a dream

Chapter 1

Living a Dream

Did you ever try to do something that was very hard? Think about learning to ride a bicycle or to catch and throw a ball. Did you have to work every day? Were you able to do it at last?

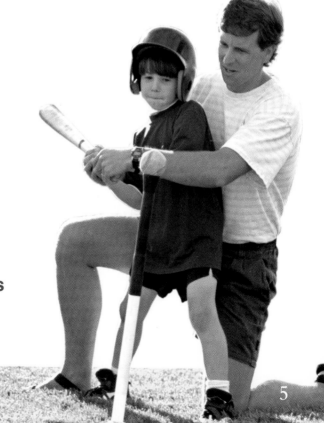

A father helps his son learn to bat a ball.

A young player catches a ball.

Lots of people work hard to do something because they have a dream. Ball players have to learn how to throw, catch, and hit a ball. Ice skaters learn to jump and spin. It takes hard work to make a dream come true.

The people you will read about dreamed of winning. At first, winning was not easy for any of them. They never gave up.

Summer Sanders is a champion swimmer. There was a time when she could not swim. Michael Jordan is known around the world as a basketball player. He could not always play well. Kristi Yamaguchi is a champion ice skater. She worked hard for many years to learn to skate.

Summer Sanders

Michael Jordan

Kristi Yamaguchi

Sammy Sosa is a famous baseball player. Like anyone else, he had to learn to throw, catch, and hit a ball.

Michael Jordan, Kristi Yamaguchi, Sammy Sosa, and Summer Sanders are all dreamers. They worked hard and kept trying. Then one day each of them could say, "I am the best."

Sammy Sosa

Sports Fact

Some skaters live their dream when they are very young. Tara Lipinski was 15 years old when she won an Olympic gold medal.

Chapter 2

Summer Sanders

Swimmers from all over the world take part in the Olympic games. Summer Sanders is one of those champion swimmers. Yet Summer did not like the water the first time she tried swimming.

Summer, 4, swam with the Roseville Sugar Bears.

Summer was two when her father built a pool in their backyard in Roseville, California. Her parents wanted her to learn to swim. Then she would be safe in the water.

Summer did not like swimming lessons. She cried at every one. Then one day Summer just jumped into the water. She showed everyone she could swim!

Summer, 13, was with the California Capital Aquatics

In college, Summer rode a bike to stay in shape.

Summer joined swim teams in school.
To be on a team, Summer had to find
time to practice swimming. She also had
to make sure she got her schoolwork done.
Summer worked very hard. She began to
win many races.

In college, Summer began to dream of being in the Olympic games. This dream made her swim even harder. Only the best swimmers could go to the games.

Finally Summer made it to the Olympic games in 1992. She was 19. She won four medals. The medals were two golds, a silver, and a bronze. Summer's dream had come true.

Summer Sanders swimming in the 1992 Olympic

Today Summer is on television. She works with the new Nickelodeon channel *Games and Sports for Kids*, or GAS. Summer likes helping kids find a dream. She helps them work hard to make their dreams come true.

Summer is on the GAS channel.

Sports Fact

Olympic games are held every two years. The summer and winter games take turns.

Chapter 3

Michael Jordan

Many people say Michael Jordan is the best basketball player ever. He never dreamed he would be a champion while growing up in North Carolina. His feet got in the way when he bounced the ball. His dream then was just to get the ball through the net.

Michael Jordan (center) started playing baseball when he was about 7.

14

Michael (center), 15, with his baseball team

Michael and his older brother, Larry, played basketball together all the time. At first Larry was a much better basketball player than Michael. He always beat Michael.

Michael decided he would play baseball if he couldn't beat Larry at basketball. He became a great pitcher. He also tried football.

Michael (back) with his family, from the left, Ronnie James, Roslyn, Deloris and Larry

Sports became a big part of Michael's life. His mother and father let him play only if he did well in school. Homework came first.

Michael and Larry still played basketball for fun. They played on a court their father had made in the backyard. Soon Michael began to beat his brother.

In high school Michael tried out for the school's top basketball team. He was not picked for the team. Other players were better. Michael also was too short. This did not stop him from trying even harder.

Michael in high school

Michael playing in college

Michael had grown 5 inches by his third year in high school. He was also a better basketball player. Finally he was picked for the top team. He became the star. He was a star basketball player in college, too.

Michael began to dream of playing in professional sports. In professional sports the players are paid to play. Michael wanted to be a professional basketball player.

Michael was picked to play with the Chicago Bulls in his last year in college. He played with the Bulls for 13 years. He helped his team win six championships.

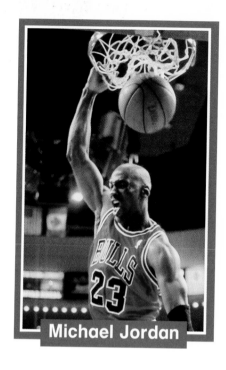
Michael Jordan

Michael in action with the Bulls

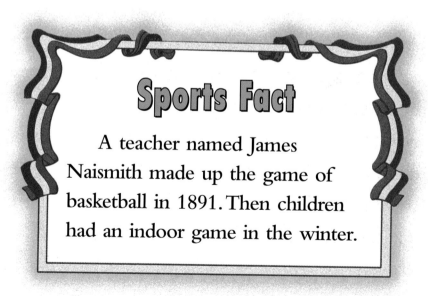

Sports Fact

A teacher named James Naismith made up the game of basketball in 1891. Then children had an indoor game in the winter.

Chapter 4

Kristi Yamaguchi

Kristi Yamaguchi was born with feet that turned in. For two years, she wore casts and braces on her feet to straighten them. No one would have guessed she would be a world champion ice skater.

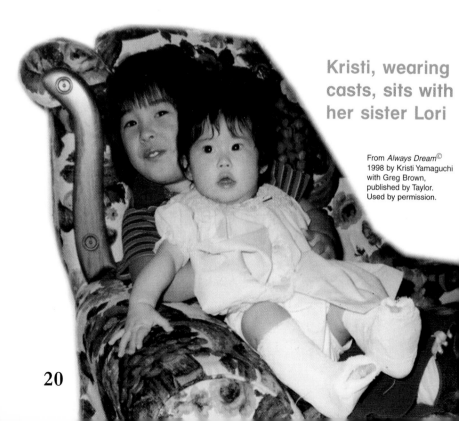

Kristi, wearing casts, sits with her sister Lori

From *Always Dream*©
1998 by Kristi Yamaguchi
with Greg Brown,
published by Taylor.
Used by permission.

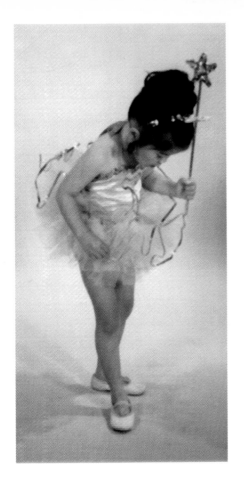

Kristi in dance class when she was 4

From *Always Dream*© 1998 by Kristi Yamaguchi with Greg Brown, published by Taylor. Used by permission.

When Kristi was four, she went to dance classes with her sister Lori. Their parents thought the classes would help Kristi's feet.

One day Kristi went to an ice-skating rink close to her home. She loved the way the skaters seemed to dance on the ice. That was when Kristi knew she wanted to skate.

Kristi asked her parents to let her take skating lessons. Her mother said that she had to start school and learn to read first. Kristi ran to her mother after her first day of school. She said, "I can read! Now can I go skating?"

Kristi's mother saw how much Kristi wanted to skate. So they went to the skating rink. Her mother held Kristi up by the arms. They skated around the rink.

Six-year-old Kristi (front row, middle) in a skating cla

From *Always Dream*© 1998 by Kristi Yamaguchi with Greg Brown, published by Taylor. Used by permission.

Kristi in skating costume at age 7

Kristi started skating lessons soon after her first visit to the rink. She skated in an ice show with her class when she was 7. That same year, Kristi was in her first skating contest. She won!

At 17, Kristi skated in the United States Olympic festival.

Kristi worked very hard on her skating as the years passed. She practiced before school. She won more skating contests. By the time she was 16, Kristi had won two junior championships. She began to dream of going to the Olympic games.

In 1992 Kristi was 20. That year she was chosen to skate in the Olympics in France. There she won the gold medal! Her dream had come true.

Today Kristi stars in ice shows around the world. She has also written a book for children called *Always Dream*. In the book Kristi tells how she became a great skater.

Kristi Yamaguchi

Kristi is now a professional skater.

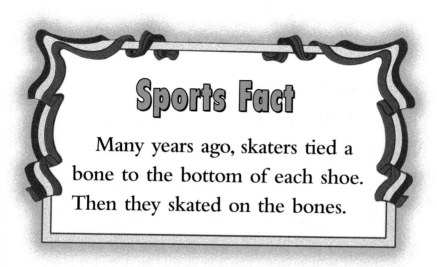

Sports Fact

Many years ago, skaters tied a bone to the bottom of each shoe. Then they skated on the bones.

Chapter 5

Sammy Sosa

Sammy Sosa is a champion baseball player. Even as a child, Sammy knew how to work hard for something he wanted. He worked to help feed his family before he worked hard at baseball.

The Dominican Republic is on an island.

Boys earning money in Santo Domingo, Dominican Republic

Sammy grew up in a country called the Dominican Republic. When he was seven, his father died. Sammy had four brothers and two sisters. His family was very poor.

Every day Sammy earned money for his family. He shined shoes. He sold oranges and newspapers. He also washed cars. He never dreamed of becoming one of the world's best baseball players. He only dreamed of helping his family.

27

When Sammy was 14, his brother told him that baseball could be a way to earn money. Sammy might be able to play with a big American team if he became a good player.

Sammy and his brother practiced hard. They used tree branches for bats and a rolled-up sock for a ball. They turned a milk carton inside out to make a glove.

Many boys play baseball in the Dominican Republ

Sammy Sosa as a Texas Ranger

Sammy worked hard for two years. Then in 1985 Sammy met a man named Omar Minaya. Minaya asked Sammy to try out for a team called the Texas Rangers. Minaya saw that Sammy could become a good player. He asked Sammy to join the team. Minaya gave him $3,500.

Sammy had never seen so much money. He bought a bicycle. Then he gave the rest of the money to his mother.

Sammy began playing for a team called the Chicago White Sox in 1989. Sammy did not do well at first. He kept trying. The White Sox finally sent him to the Chicago Cubs. On that team, Sammy became one of the greatest baseball players ever.

Sammy's best year was in 1998. He hit a record 66 home runs. Sammy was named Most Valuable Player even though another player hit more home runs.

Sammy hits his record 66th home run.

Sammy's dream to help his family had finally come true. At the same time, Sammy found another dream. He became a great baseball player.

Sammy in action with the Chicago Cubs

Sammy Sosa

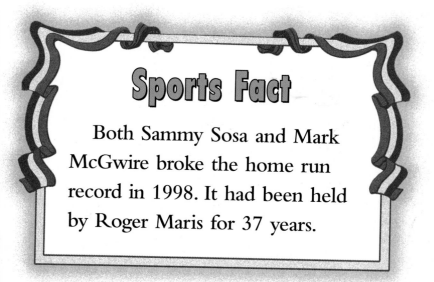

Sports Fact

Both Sammy Sosa and Mark McGwire broke the home run record in 1998. It had been held by Roger Maris for 37 years.

GLOSSARY

cast [kast] material that hardens when wrapped around a broken bone

champion [CHAM pee un] being the best of its kind

home run [hohm run] a hit in baseball when a player runs around all the bases to score a point

medal [MEH dul] a flat piece of metal given as a prize

pitcher [PIH chur] a baseball player who throws the ball to the batter

professional [pruh FESH uh nul] being paid to play a sport or do a job

record [REH kurd] the best yet done

rink [rihnk] a building with a sheet of ice for skating